T0064094

Bill Overmyer has authored three books.

OVER THE ROAD TRUCK DRIVING POEMS

A collection of poems related to the trials and tribulations of the over the road truck drivers.

THE DEAD CAT BOUNCE

A detailed description of the bottom of a severe stock market decline. This work will enable a first time investor to develop the skills to assess the correct time to buy and sell stock and realize an amazing profit within one year.

BRONZE MINER

This romance novel takes place in a remote mountain town. The shared interests between the two lovers are a bronze foundry work place, a recreational ski area, the great outdoors and a student parachute center.

OVER THE ROAD TRUCK DRIVER POEMS

BY BILL OVERMYER

OVER THE ROAD TRUCK DRIVER POEMS

iUniverse books may be ordered through booksellers or by contacting:

iUniverse
1663 Liberty Drive
Bloomington, IN 47403
www.iuniverse.com
844-349-9409

ISBN: 978-1-4917-4850-3 (sc)
ISBN: 978-1-4917-4851-0 (e)

Library of Congress Control Number: 2014917295

Print information available on the last page.

iUniverse rev. date: 09/06/2022

This book is dedicated to over

the road truck drivers, to those dedicated people

who keep them rolling, to those who bring in the new

drivers, and to all men and women who serve in the Armed

Forces of the United States of America.

Acknowledgements

Special thanks to Sean Shannon, Jim Zubia and

Felton Cotton – The Captain

Andrew and William Jones

the Red Shirts and Adrian.

CONTENTS

PROLOGUE

1   DAY OF ARRIVAL

5   DO I EVER THINK OF YOU?

7   3 AM DELIVERY

10 DRIVING GOD'S EARLY
    MORNING WAKE UP CALL

12 SOMETIMES YOU'VE GOT TO PLAY PRETEND

16 "I THINK I'M GOING DOWN!"

18 TRUCK WASH TIME

21 LATE FOR THE DOCK

23 THE GREAT DRIVERS

26 GAPER'S BLOCK

28 WELCOME TO GLARE ICE CEMETERY

30 ICY ROADS

33 LOAD 101

35 TOO MANY BATTLES

37 YES, YOUR HONOR

40 THE GREAT ATLANTA RUSH HOUR

44 I FINALLY WON THE LOTTO

46 THE COUNTY FAIR

48 FLOATING DANGER ZONE

50 THE ON RAMP MENTALITY

52 MERGING FROM THE ACCELERATION RAMP

54 CROTCH ROCKET

56 THE HEAVY MORNING MIST

58 MY STOMACH IS QUEASY

62 TRASH FOOD

65 2300 AND NO PLACE TO PARK

67 DREAMING OF THE COUNTRYSIDE

70 IMAGINARY ANGER

74 TEMPER CONTROL

76 IT'S PART OF DRIVING A BIG SEMI TRUCK

78 SPATIAL RELATIONS

80 QUICK QUIPS

82 TWO EXPLOSIONS

84 THE HIGH COST OF ANGER

87 BEHIND THE CLUSTER

89   NOTHANKYOU@REJECTION.COM

90   UP ON THE ROAD HE STOOD

92   BIG DELIVERY

95   WAKE UP HOSPITAL

97   MR COCHISE MOUNTAIN

99   CLIMBING THE HILLS AND GOING

     DOWN THE MOUNTAINS

104 THE 72ND ANNUAL CAR SHOW

107 THE FUEL MANAGER

EPILOGUE

113 THE WOOD STOVE

APPENDIX

115 THE ENRAGED STUDENT AND

     THE DRIVING INSTRUCTOR

PROLOGUE

In my dreams forever.

For a week or two, I pray

that I get to spend with you

three or four whole days.

I also pray that the sunshine will hold

for three or four days,

as I make my way back to our home

and back to you.

For us that is not enough.

Not enough of you for me.

Not enough of me for you.

For the last four hundred miles I have seen

miles upon miles of green,

gold and light brown fields,

and stately farm houses.

The road ever upward.

The hill always rising

until I reach the top

and then the peaks of the Rockies

appear in front of me,

left to right as far as I can see.

The sun is up in the east as I head to our house.

The painted white dashes lead the way,

and mark the road to our home

where we live and pray, and plan to stay.

I chase the shadow of the truck down the highway.

There is not a care in the world going my way.

I am anxious for the moments I have missed,

and anxious to be by your side,

to share your loving kiss.

DAY OF ARRIVAL

He still has three hours to go.

The clouds had built up in the mountains.

He parked the big rig in the company yard

as a new storm was moving in.

He still has a few more things to do

before he is finally through.

He finished his qual com driver log.

He selected "off duty" and typed in the truck location.

He switched to the communication menu

and left a freeform message

for his driver manager, Andrew.

He would be off four days and return on the fifth.

Next he moved the master electric switch

to the off position.

This would protect the batteries from going low.

He grabbed his carry all bag that he packed

two days ago.

He placed it in the bed

of his second hand pickup.

He paid $600 for the pickup, eleven years ago.

The only things that don't work are the power windows.

After the tractor doors were shut,

he climbed into his old, beat up, pickup

and began the one hour drive home.

The clouds had drifted out of the mountains and

covered the town with overcast by the time he

arrived at their house.

He turned into the driveway and there on the front

porch swing was his sweetheart.

She was waiting for him in all of her beauty and loyalty.

She waved to him and she hollered,

"My truck driver is home!"

He fetched his bag from the truck bed

as Fritz bolted off the porch.

They jumped up and down together, pushed and

shoved, barked and nipped at one another.

"Hey, there! Do you recognize me?

I'm your old girlfriend!

Fritz has saved a warm spot for you,

on our front porch swing.

It happens to be right here beside me."

"That will do fine, sweet one. I will be right there.

I am very anxious to see you. I want to sit and talk with

you while I unwind." He lofted a snowball to Fritz. Fritz

lept high in the air. He snapped his jaws and the

snowball disappeared.

"Come sit here and hold my hand.

We can stay warm together under our blanket."

He stepped up onto the porch and they shared a tender

kiss. "Yes my love. I am finally here. What is

it you desire?"

"After you relax you can tell me where you've been.

Tell me all of the news. The worst and the best.

Tell me the good and the bad.

Then I will know just how to take care of you

and nourish you. Do I have the usual four days?"

He sat beside her on the swing

and they wrapped the blanket around them.

"Of course, my love, and I have the usual exciting tales

to tell you, and here is the first one.

When I'm out on the road I think of you every morning,

every afternoon and every night."

DO I EVER THINK OF YOU?

I think of you when I'm shaving.

I look in the mirror

and I imagine I see,

your warm smile, and your eyes

looking back at me.

I want to get my face nice and smooth,

because I miss you.

I'm looking out for that special kiss

that is only delivered by your sweet lips.

I know you like a nice clean shave,

so your lips and cheeks can glide

smoothly around my face.

To prove to you my love is true,

I want my face irresistible to you,

so I can live in bliss.

When you dance around me

to place a quick kiss,

this tells me that you love me.

Then I can't resist

the urge to kiss you back

strongly and deeply

with the love and commitment

that binds us together completely.

"That is the biggest tale I have, dear.

Would you care to hear more?"

She threw her arms around his neck and gave him the

long, sweet kiss that he was praying for.

When she was through, she answered,

"I adore you and love you more than anyone.

And yes, I want to hear more."

He smiled and said, "Okay. Here we go.

I will tell you the first of many tales.

Please sit back and relax, and I will put you to sleep with

my endless adventures, far before I am finished."

3 AM DELIVERY

There's a three am delivery this morning.

I'm creeping along the road.

My four way flashers are on.

No one else has come along.

I'm all alone, and it is peaceful.

Everything is quiet except for the qual com.

It is flashing a little red light.

And it is telling me of my plight.

I have exceeded my ten hours of drive time.

"You are out of driving hours!"

"You are out of driving hours!"

The day is starting off great,

as I turn toward the warehouse gate.

I'm half an hour early. I'm just ahead of schedule.

The security man can't mark me late.

I turned the volume down as he approached.

He inquired,

"What's that flashing red light?"

I replied,

"Oh, that is just a bloke,

who wants to talk with me. He can wait.

You have my attention. Sir,

I'm here to deliver

forty four thousand pounds

of beef and liver."

"Door number four and make it fast.

Trailer tandems all the way back.

We'll get you unloaded right away.

Then you can be on your way,

to your new assignment

before the sun comes up today."

"I'm mighty grateful, Boss.

Usually, I have to wait."

He replied, "Not today my friend.

Let me get the gate."

I rolled on through and down the row of doors.

It wasn't long before I found number four.

I slid the tandems back, I opened the trailer doors.

Then I slowly rolled back

and docked on door number four.

DRIVING GOD'S EARLY MORNING WAKE UP CALL

O five hundred is the time to roll

down the highway in the early morning,

whether the weather is clear or storming.

The sky is a slight gray overcast.

The light drops of moisture

from the cool of the night

coalesce on the windscreen

and reflect the oncoming headlights.

The early morning drive is the way to survive.

Gone is the glare of approaching headlights

that wash our vision out.

Gone are the speeding cars

racing and darting about.

Slowly the oncoming sun

burns a hole through the thin shroud of cloud.

A sun beam of solid might

turns the gray sky to a light white.

It strikes the hillside in front of me

with an intense arc of bright light.

A few moments later

a blinding sun crests the horizon.

Its light marches steadily forward

from behind me to the world in front of me.

It removes the morning gray

and it lights up this brand new day.

And God has kissed the morning awake.

SOMETIMES YOU'VE GOT TO PLAY PRETEND

Day after day. Night after night.

I spend all of my time,

eating, sleeping and driving

in this cab. It is so bad,

that sometimes I think

I'm a rat in a lab.

It's small and it's cramped.

I feel like I am

a sardine in a can,

a chicken in a coop,

or a squirrel in a nest.

This condition has totally turned me into a crab.

When I get home for four days

I will be very glad.

Day in, day out and night time too.

I easily get bored and blue.

So sometimes to mentally get away,

I climb up into the crow's nest,

and pretend I'm a pirate, on a hot windy day.

I know I will be rewarded with a gold doubloon,

if I can find a ship to scuttle soon.

So you see,

there is plenty of adventure

out here on the road,

if only you allow your mind to unfold.

Sometimes I'm the captain.

Sometimes I'm the cook,

or the gunner to fire the cannon.

I can imagine so many things to get me away.

You see, drivers don't often have enough time to play.

The other trucks that pass me by

are actually silver ships filled with gold and supplies.

They too are like ships on the high seas.

So let's break these chains and mutiny!

Listen closely and you might hear,

"Ship Ahoy!"

"The men are starving, Captain."

"There is mutiny in the air!"

You must be bold!

Kick Compliance and Dispatch

down into the hold.

Now hoist Jolly Roger

and give them the canon broadside!

Blow her to smithereens

to feed the sardines!

Prepare to board and plunder

and take her 40,000 pounds of goods.

Her treasure will be ours

to barter and trade.

And we will have food again

the next time we pull into harbor

and play pretend

at the high seas travel center.

"I THINK I'M GOING DOWN!"

The call came out clear and loud over the CB

just east of Oklahoma City on Interstate 40.

A truck driver, in a big Swift rig,

swerved onto the off ramp.

His heart had skipped a beat

and it was trying to cramp.

He didn't panic, he knew what was going on.

He grabbed his cell phone and dialed 911.

He remained calm and he stayed mentally strong,

He explained to the operator where he was

and what had gone wrong.

The EMT'S placed him on a gurney

for the short journey

to the ambulance emergency room.

There might be a chance to save him,

if they got him resuscitated soon.

If he was unconscious, I will bet to this day,

that a smile was on his face.

Because you know,

when God calls we answer.

Especially if it's time to go.

Even then we smile because we know.

There will be no more torture or

ten hour days of driving.

For now we will log all of our working hours

in the Kingdom of God's heavenly towers.

TRUCK WASH TIME

A small thunder shower approached

and it appeared that

things were going to get a little damp.

So on the spur of the moment

I turned onto the exit ramp.

An idea occurred to me

to make this rain shower a special occasion.

Besides, it was way past time

to step outside and get some circulation.

I pulled a sponge and a bucket

out of the passenger side box,

along with some water and soap.

Because my bright idea

was to wash the truck

and save a dollar, I hoped.

It was just a drizzle at first.

I lathered up the cab with a lot of soap.

I really didn't care if I got soaked.

I soaped up the doors,

the bumper and the windshield too.

The fuel tanks and the hood,

as far as I could reach,

and everything was looking good.

When I finished,

I climbed the steps and sat in the cab.

I slid the key in the ignition.

I started the engine

and engaged the transmission.

I returned to the highway, soap suds and all.

Several trucks passed me by

as I merged the Soap Suds Express

to the highway from the on ramp.

And all the drivers were staring back

with wide open eyes.

A hard rain began after a little while,

and that rain gave me a satisfied smile.

The rain washed all the soap suds away.

And when the suds were gone

the truck was sparkling clean.

And I knew the best thing about it was

it was all for free.

LATE FOR THE DOCK

I have 282 miles to the warehouse dock.

I have six and a half hours of driving

left on the clock.

And while I am winding through this city,

what do I find?

A big traffic jam that will leave me

two hours behind.

It is an exciting accident, so let's all stop and gape.

Never mind if it will make anyone late.

Here we are. It's all stop and go,

and the TV station works

to get the carnage on a video.

This jam is caused by a bunch of lugs,

as every car in line stops

to look for some blood.

If they would mind their own business

and keep the traffic flowing,

the rest of us could move on

and get to where we're going.

They need to let the drama and trauma pass.

Then all of us could clear the obstacle twice as fast.

Now I'm late for my appointment.

I will be late to the dock.

I'll be rescheduled tomorrow,

and that is just my luck.

And it is all because of

this stupid gapers' block.

THE GREAT DRIVERS

In two thousand and three

the IRS was after me.

So, like a run away mouse,

I boarded up the house.

I took off for the highway

and a special place to hide out.

I joined the truckers merrily.

Unlike the quitters

or the lazy people in our society,

I felt this move would make a real man of me.

It would give me a paycheck.

I could forego the food stamps.

I could be proud once again.

I could lift my head high

and not have to be a tramp.

Little did I know how tough it would be

to drive a huge truck.

A driver has to be stout of mind and gut,

and the driver can never, never give up.

Drivers have no feeling of doubt or defeat.

Their attitudes and manners

are like steel and concrete.

They are proud to make a contribution.

They do not stay home and pout.

Altogether, tis their discipline, pride and courage,

that really helps them out.

They only have ten hours a day to drive.

They have to think smart to survive

and make it to the warehouse dock on time.

They have to be smart and fix their problems quick,

especially, if it's a mechanical glitch.

Drivers always deal with contingencies and constraints.

Their driver managers hear all of the complaints.

They are overwhelmed with government rules

and regulations,

but together they solve their problems

and bad situations.

There are a hundred things they have to do.

to get through their trials and daily snafus.

When no one else is there to help a driver out,

the driver is on his own

to find a remedy or some way out.

When no one can imagine the trials and complications,

the drivers use their own brains and imaginations

to solve their problems and tough situations.

GAPER'S BLOCK

Only idiots slow down to look at car wrecks.

They love to twist around and turn their necks.

Some come to a full stop so they can stare.

Even when police wave them through with a glare.

They search for an accident victim,

so they can scream,

"That man lost his leg."

"Oh, my gosh!"

"Look at how much he bled!"

After all, they have waited in line

and they have paid their dues.

Now it is their turn to check out the view.

They stop to stare at those in pain,

and the unfortunate ones who have been maimed.

I think these lookie loos

are all insane.

Now I sometimes wish it was

the other way around

and the viewer could be lying there on the ground.

Let it be their turn to lay in agony and pain,

while lookie loo after lookie loo

rolled by again and again.

They have no regard for the destinations or deadlines

of the people in line behind them.

The have the view and the "now,"

and they are ignorant of the traffic

piled up behind them.

WELCOME TO GLARE ICE CEMETERY

Welcome to glare ice cemetery.

It is slick as snot on the road you see.

Don't you dare move the wheel or you might pitch,

your truck onto its side and into a ditch.

There is no recovery.

There is no escape.

If you let it happen,

then you have chosen your fate.

When the moisture and temperature cool at 32

degrees,

then you have the makings of

the Glare Ice Cemetery.

There is no escape. There is no hope

to magically steer along this slippery slope.

Even the most skilled drivers alive,

cannot drive for very long

on snow and ice and survive.

There is no sense to carry on for a thrill

Don't think that everyone

will be impressed with your skill.

If you continue to drive and try to play hero,

then you may end up as big as a zero.

It won't help anyone if you crash your boat.

The EMT's will find you in the cab,

at the end of your rope,

in the Glare Ice Cemetery on the side of the slope.

ICY ROADS

The icy roads cannot be beat.

You must realize that and accept the defeat.

Hold dear the need to stay alive.

Park the truck in time, so you can survive.

Remember that tomorrow the sun will shine.

Resume your quest then, while in the meantime,

call your driver manager and tell him

you are going on break,

and you will be sleeping in.

Then as an aside remind the guy

to please reschedule your delivery time.

If he reads you the riot act,

then explain to him that one day

he will receive your payback.

At your request, this can be done you see.

Because it is impossible to move

80,000 pounds over snow and ice safely.

Why creep along at twenty miles an hour or less

when you could have a couple of hours rest?

Then you will be ready when the roads are clear,

and the truck and trailer will be easy to steer.

Suddenly, you will feel nothing but cheer.

You can drive the roads with confidence

and not with fear.

When you leave the snowstorm you must do it in time.

Before that crucial window arrives, all is fine.

You can drive on through bad weather,

if you feel inclined.

But please keep in mind,

once the storm intensifies,

you have run out of time.

So find a safe harbor and park,

so you can unwind.

The snow will completely ruin your day.

It will cover all the glass and block all the light away.

Your windshield will be a blindfold of gray so drab.
that the dark of night will appear inside your cab.

Should you decide to play hero and continue to drive,
then your truck will be sliding to the end of the ride.
Possibly, you could end up resting on your side.
And a concussion or death might be your new bride.

It will take many days to move the truck
and place you in a grave.
All of the paper work will be around
for three hundred sixty days.
The equipment cannot be salvaged,
and you know the company ways.
They will bury you in the trailer lot
out in front of the company shop.
Then everyone can stop
to pay tribute to you
and spit on your grave.

LOAD 101

Heading east out of Holcomb Kansas on Highway 156,

everything is a green field since we left the city.

The temperature is 70 and there is no humidity.

Only one other person on the highway do I see,

as old number 57, a tanker, catches up to me.

Together we drive along this two lane road peacefully.

Our windows are down to catch the cool breeze.

As the evening sun sets behind us,

it casts our truck shadows out in front.

And we begin to play

follow the leader down the highway.

A curve to the right throws our shadows out

to the left side of our trucks.

And the shadows grow to twice the size of us.

They are the shape of large loaves of bread,

as we race each other down the freeway,

running head to head.

Our shadows race each other side by side

and we are mesmerized by the simple,

yet artistic, marking of the dotted lines.

And as we negotiate another curve again,

the shadow of the mirror on the passenger side

traces the solid white shoulder line

perfectly through the curve.

TOO MANY BATTLES

Too many battles along life's trails.

To many trials with too many fails.

This eventually erodes the resilience that we need

to deal with most of life's uncertainties.

It doesn't hurt to loose just a few.

We can usually recover and start anew.

But once in a while you will see

someone who has lost one too many.

Each new encounter can produce a small loss.

As the number of losses add up over time,

this will cause some of us to lose our minds.

Then we become focused too much on the battle.

We too often bark when we are rattled.

We are always on the defense against hostility,

and this new demeanor overwhelms

our normal personality.

We begin to bark and snap at the slightest misgiving.

Hatred now controls all of our thinking.

Just a small push will send our heads spinning

into a downward spiral,

with dark thoughts of never winning.

So have sympathy and help us before it's too late.

Do something of kindness that we will appreciate.

Please! Never mention these despicable words to us.

Driver Manager, Dispatch or Compliance.

YES, YOUR HONOR

They dragged me out of my cab.

I was kicking and screaming,

and I was fighting mad.

And in my face

they emptied a can of mace.

They clubbed my elbows and my knees.

So I fell to the ground,

and covered my head.

Right there on the concrete, I rested and bled.

They cuffed me and shoved me

onto the back of a black and white.

And then they drove me downtown

to visit the ornery Judge Brown.

Judge Brown stared down at me.

"Have you been driving recklessly?"

Then he shouted, "Answer me!"

I knew he was planning to throw the book at me.

I heard myself answer,

"Yes, your Honor. I must confess.

In the last six months, I would guess,

I have run ten to fifteen vehicles onto the

shoulder.

And four of them were big yellow school buses in

Boulder."

I heard myself say,

"I could hear the screams of those snot nose kids.

I wish I had seen the tears

in their eyes and the fear

on their faces."

The judge stood up and he hollered,

"You lose your license,

and you pay us fifty thousand dollars!"

It was just then that my mouth fell open

and I realized that I had to roll over

and find my alarm clock

so I could shut the thing off

and start the day over.

THE GREAT ATLANTA RUSH HOUR

I got a wide open lane in front of me.

so I can stop my big truck easily.

But it looks like I will continue to suffer,

as these cars continue to steal my safety buffer.

Mentally, these fools are trying to figure out

what they will do and say at their jobs today,

right here in rush hour, on the Atlanta freeway.

Looks like I got here at the wrong time,

as we circle Atlanta on I 285.

All of a sudden out in front

a line for an exit has traffic piled up.

The cars around me swerve recklessly

for the far left lane as each tries in vain,

to merge over into the fast lane.

They make the Daytona 500 look tame.

Once past the exit the traffic has dispersed.

The next move these semi-conscious

extremists have rehearsed.

They step on the gas and they all speed away.

It's time to get going, and get on with their day.

They jockey another mile down the road

and they find

the traffic is backed up again

due to an accident this time.

It's just another bottleneck!

They slow down and merge to get around the wreck.

And once past the accident all three lanes

open up wide again.

They swerve and dart ahead just to gain one length.

They think they have gained some time,

when in a thirty minute drive they might save five.

But is it really worth the risk, if you want to stay alive?

Their minds are so dulled from this routine

that they fall right back into the swing of things.

But it will only be a matter of time

until they reach for something or other.

They will drive through the next long curve

and discover,

there's a jam up front and they can't recover.

Red lights flash out a warning

as the drivers hit their brakes.

If the cars are too close, then it is too late.

Now it is only fate.

With the car bumper in front of them,

they have a date.

Then all at once they stop with a crash,

and the impact throws them into the dash.

Out pops the plastic airbag barely in time

to keep their jaw bones and necks properly aligned.

The sounds of the smash.

The pounding of the metal.

The rain shower of glass.

Their bodies are mangled from injuries.

And all the cussing and the obscenities

are embedded forever into their memories.

This is the spirit of rush hour you see.

The drivers create their fate

whenever they leave the house to late.

Like maniacs they speed relentlessly

to be on time at the factory.

So next time you are late in the Atlanta rush hour,

remember this story and try to slow down.

Please leave me in in the beauty of my open lane,

unless you want to be run over

by my small freight train.

I FINALLY WON
THE LOTTO

I finally won the lotto.

My head is in the clouds.

I didn't win ten million,

but I've enough to spread around.

I'm giving some to Mother.

I'm giving some to Dad,

for putting up with

all the grief I caused

when I was just a lad.

I didn't win ten million.

I only won one half.

I think I'll pay my credit cards

and all the bills I have.

No more mortgage payment.

Finally! At last!

Living hand to mouth each month

is something in the past.

I will continue to go to work

just to rub it in.

And finally my wife and I

can fall in love again.

THE COUNTY FAIR

It's a beauty of a day.

I wish there was a place to park this rig.

I'd buy a general admission ticket

and go right on in.

I'd walk down the lanes between the booths

just to stretch my legs.

I might even take a ride or two

and reminisce about the day

I kissed a girl on the ferris wheel

and felt the G's on the tilt a wheel.

or scared a girl in the haunted house

just pretending I was a mouse.

There is fun for all ages.

Everyone is here.

The kids run wild.

Excitement builds in their eyes.

Knock a kewpie doll over

and win your girl a prize.

I'd like to see the bucking broncos

and the barrel racing.

And before I was all through,

I would probably buy some food.

Bratwurst or turkey.

Maybe even a little beef jerky.

Of course this would require

a liquid refreshment or two,

to wash it all down,

along with the excitement

and the atmosphere at the county fair.

This is what I would like to do.

But it cannot happen.

As fate has it,

the usual delivery is almost due.

FLOATING DANGER ZONE

In front of the truck is my great big safety space.

It's all for me, so stay out of my place.

Please show some consideration for me.

Because this empty space is really the key

to help me keep my sanity.

Stay out of my space

and don't disturb my pace.

Don't disturb my beauty.

Don't disturb my vision.

Or my truck and I

might put you in remission.

Stay out of my way cause I can't stop.

If you are in front of me, then your car will be the mop

and I will use your car to clear a path through

any cars that are piled up in front of you.

Just leave me in in the beauty of my open lane.

Don't mess with me 'cause I can't guarantee

that I will stop in time

to save your pretty car from a tragedy.

THE ON RAMP
MENTALITY

They should be paying attention.

They should be adjusting their speed,

so they can find an opening

and slip into the flowing stream

of traffic congestion.

If they don't look until the last second,

then they are out of luck.

They just about have heart failure,

when they see my great big truck.

I slow down

and they slow down,

which leaves us side by side.

If they reach the end of the access ramp

they will really be in for a ride.

If they drive onto the shoulder,

then they will have to cope

with the guard rail right beside them.

Then they will realize ramp merging is no joke.

So step on the gas and step on the brake.

They would be better off on roller skates.

They are at the end of the acceleration lane.

They didn't do their job,

and I am not to blame.

Show me the law that says I have to pull over.

It looks like they will get the shoulder.

Watch out for the guard rail on the passenger side.

They will talk at home about me for quite some time.

They cuss me and they curse me.

They even flip me the finger.

It indicates their inability

to negotiate a ramp to highway merger.

MERGING FROM THE ACCELERATION RAMP

Here they come.

In the morning sun.

They are gliding down the ramp

Is it all just for fun?

They use the mirrors

to put on lipstick and skin cream.

Do they look to the left?

Are you kidding me?

These folks are in denial.

They are floating along in a dream.

They are putting on makeup and shaving their chins.

Man, what a mess they have put me in.

They expect me to produce a space

so they can merge right in.

But I can't do that if I am all boxed in.

And all they do is wave and grin!

Sometimes all at once, as if in a horror show,

they come to the end of the access road.

Their signal goes on

and their head snaps to the left.

They look at the front of my bumper,

and they squeeze right in.

They miss my front bumper

by the hair on their chin.

But they never feel guilty.

They are used to scooting in.

To say I didn't scream would be a lie.

I think I left a stain on the seat that time.

These lazy merging drivers

don't even realize

that they were just an inch or two away

from losing their lives.

CROTCH ROCKET

He gunned up right beside me,

and he swerved in front gracefully.

He missed my front bumper

by about three feet.

Then he roared on down the freeway

in a burst of speed.

He was just having fun,

speeding by me 20 miles faster.

There was no doubt in my mind

that his actions would lead to disaster.

His chance to stay upright looked pretty slim,

when a motorist took the space just in front of him.

He had to swerve fast to keep from being hit.

But it was too late. He had just been clipped.

The move was so sudden his balance was lost.

It looked as if there would be no medical cost.

He threw up his hands. His heart skipped a beat.

And it looked as if he had lost his seat.

It happened so fast there was no chance to react.

He must have slid a hundred feet on his back.

Then he hit the median with quite an impact.

Every one slowed down.

Some saw him crumble.

When he hit the wall

he surely took a tumble.

There is no doubt about it.

Motorcycle wrecks are mighty gruesome.

So if you ride a motorcycle in heavy traffic,

please don't be a nuisance.

THE HEAVY
MORNING MIST

It is time for the drivers to start their day,

but the heavy morning mist

is really in their way.

They don't have three hours to wait around

for the sun to cut through

so the drivers can see the ground.

A few adventurous drivers are out.

They have their flashers on

and are rolling slowly about.

All of this may seem crazy to you

but there is a delivery of goods

in the trailer that is due.

They play a dangerous game of peek a boo,

as they scout the mist

they cannot see through.

They strain to catch a glimpse

of red tail lights in front of them,

so they won't slam into someone's rear end.

Close to the top of the hills

the mist disappears.

The sun shines through

and the roads are clear.

The trucks speed up

for a little while, but then

the road leads downhill,

and once again,

it takes the drivers back into

the thick mist that they cannot see through.

Tall black trees jump out of the gray

one at a time, like sentries,

they line the edge of the freeway,

and help guide the drivers

safely along their way.

MY STOMACH IS QUEASY

This ain't no romantic part of a play.

The ham and cheese omelet

that I ate today

did not taste quite right.

And now my intestines are having a fight.

The eggs did not have that crisp, clean taste.

They were a little sour and they tasted like paste.

And now I am grumbling

because my intestines are rumbling.

As I struggle to hold the diarrhea back,

I am convinced

that I am the victim

of a food poisoning attack.

Every man is humbled when he is searching to find

that elusive restroom which is never nearby.

So I sped to the truck stop.

I rolled right through the fuel pumps.

And once I got stopped,

I artfully unloaded myself from the truck.

I was careful not to stir up a commotion

or cause myself a sudden explosion.

I was more than frantic!

As I walked into the travel center,

I tried not to panic.

I searched for the restroom location.

I tried to appear calm

like I was on vacation.

The line of desperate drivers

snaked out from the Men's restroom.

So, to forgo the impending gloom and doom,

I ducked into the Women's restroom.

I determined two stalls were busy.

I quietly slipped into an empty one.

Hopefully, my dilemma

would soon be over and done.

My pants were no struggle.

I dropped them to the ground.

I quickly spun around, and as I sat down,

I completed my download in a heartbeat

just as my butt hit the toilet seat.

The noise was loud and deafening,

and the smell of gas was stifling.

I had made it and I was grateful.

But I couldn't believe that my bowels

sounded like an erupting volcano.

The ladies quickly finished their business.

Their stall doors flew open.

They coughed and laughed and gasped,

as they ran for their exit.

No longer daunted I quickly cleaned up.

I was happy and ready to go drive a truck.

I secured my clothing and left the stall.

The room was empty and I headed for the hall.

I washed my hands,

and I opened the door,

just as two women walked in.

They jumped back astonished

and I quickly moved past them.

The boys were hooting and laughing

as you can imagine.

But I proudly walked out

after finishing my business.

I tried to be dignified,

so I held my head high.

Once again, I was alive.

And then a thought crossed my mind.

"Better to erupt in the Women's room

than outside in the hall in the Men's line."

TRASH FOOD

Up and down the hills and around the bend,

I'm trying to save time, and so here I am,

drinking pots of coffee and eating trash food again.

The pressure of time

has caused my addiction.

I thought this condition

would never come to fruition.

I got sucked in gradually,

and I've been skipping the good meals

that I really need.

I was forced to cut corners.

but now I'm saving time.

I get more driving miles in

so I can make the delivery on time.

My ruffles, doritos,

corn chips and cheetos

are all exotic to me.

I'd rather eat them than watch TV.

I'm addicted to Little Debbie's,

chips, pizza and beef jerky.

I've gained 20 pounds.

I wish I could quit.

I wish I could go cold turkey.

Just look at me now.

It's so demeaning.

The empty chip bags are piled up to the ceiling.

They are piled so high that I can barely see

through the window and down the street.

When it's time to clean out my cab out,

I'm so lazy now,

I take the cheap and easy route.

I roll the windows down

and the wind sucks the bags out.

Here is my dilemma now.

It is a moral and ethical question.

I will be your friend forever,

if you can help me decide.

Should I just suck it up

and continue to drive?

Or, should I just give up now

and turn myself in for treatment?

2300 AND NO
PLACE TO PARK

The qual com's a flashing. The day is up.

I have thirty minutes left just to park this truck.

It is 11pm and there is not one spot

left in this whole blessed truck stop.

I will have to invent a place to back.

It is on the other side

of the mechanic shop,

in front of the huge tire rack.

Each day requires ten hours rest.

Because tomorrow, as always,

will be another day

and another test.

I will roll down the highway

and try to do my best.

Rest will keep me healthy

and I will hold a good mental attitude.

This will get me safely through the cities

to the warehouse dock

where the meat load is due.

To arrive by the appointment time,

I will do my best.

But right now

I need to get my ten hours rest.

DREAMING OF THE COUNTRYSIDE

I'm tired of the narrow lanes

on the city interstates.

I'm tired of all of the anxiety

that they create.

I'm tired of all the congestion,

and lots of other things

that are too numerous to mention.

Let's roll on out of this big city

to the beautiful countryside.

Where life is free and easy

and the driving time is fine.

The rivers here are cool

and if I had the time,

I would fashion a fishing pole

from a tree branch

with my old rusty knife.

I would sit comfortably on the river bank

and stretch my legs.

I would begin to reminisce and unwind

I might even drink a little wine.

I would fish until I caught three.

Then of course, I'd skin 'em and clean 'em.

I would drop them fillets into a frying pan

and cook 'em.

Then I would put those delicious fillets

on my plate and I would eat 'em.

I would place my folding chair

by a big rock.

And if the blazing sun got too hot,

then I would sit in the shade of a tree

where the squirrels could drop

their twigs on me.

With the day's glow upon me

I would just think and reflect

of all the wonderful blessings

that we have on earth

and all of the wonderful things that we get to see,

the beauty that God has given to you and to me.

Each day is a pearl

and it is up to us to make it the best we can.

We should believe and trust in God's serenity.

We should believe and have hope for our families.

IMAGINARY ANGER

I have to let it all go

It's madness don't you see?

No matter what it was that ticked me off.

No matter how mad about it I got.

If someone says something wrong to you,

do you try to get back?

Do you try to attack?

Do you want to get even?

Sure you do. It is a hard fact.

But why bother,

when it is only smiles and courtesy that they lack?

You've done no one wrong.

They have done it to you all along.

Now you are ready to explode with rage,

just because someone has rattled your cage.

Someone has finally gotten under your skin,

and *you* have planted an imaginary fantasy within.

That fantasy is locked on an argument in your head

of what you should have done

or what you should have said.

And like a child you will agonize over it endlessly.

You act it out in your mind

until the ending, to you, is satisfactory.

But in this fruitless mental game,

all rationality will be drained away.

And you will miss the visual cues

outside your windscreen

of all that's going on around you.

Because the only item left in your brain

is the anger and resentment

that is driving you insane.

You have to get used to it.

You have to grow up and be a better trucker.

You can't go on much longer

dwelling in imaginary anger.

What you have to do

is figure out how to

end this meaningless bout

before it gets started, no doubt.

You have to say something

to snuff little petty fires out

before they begin, my friend.

I'll give you a tip.

The answer here is the quick quip.

You have to believe they will work.

You have to present them with confidence

to quell the jerks.

They have to be practical

for them to work.

Quips work best

when they are pre planned

and practiced ahead of time

in your verbal mind.

So practice them

until they become automatic.

Here are just a few

that will throw your adversary into a panic.

These will easily get you started.

"You are obviously retarded."

"How did you ever get a license to drive a truck?"

"I've got more important things to do

than to waste my time listening or messing with you."

"Maybe you've got your panties in a bunch?

Why don't you change them when you go to lunch?"

"You are such a dope.

You need to rinse your mouth out with soap."

"Why don't you take a hike

and go fly a kite?"

Sometimes our skins are just too thin

The only solution for us is to shape up.

So acquire some quick quips,

use them and good luck.

TEMPER CONTROL

I have to learn to control my temper.

I have to learn to let go of the anger.

I have to realize that the big truck I'm driving

is an obstacle to the tiny cars behind me.

I have to understand

at a very slow speeds,

the car drivers will continue

to squeeze and weave,

hastily, all around me.

I've really been kind to them here

by not profiling or calling them names.

But 99 % of truckers agree

that car drivers are insane.

They are all a bunch of flakes.

They believe that all it takes

to stop an 80,000 pound truck

is to jam a heavy foot

on the brakes.

And then the truck will stop

as fast as a kid on roller skates.

IT'S PART OF DRIVING A BIG SEMI TRUCK

It's part of driving a big semi truck.

You can never, never, never give up.

You have to keep your cool.

You have to slow down

and brake for these fools.

But what really aggravates me

is when they cut in front of me at a slower speed

and miss my bumper

by less than 20 feet.

They cut in front of my truck

from the access ramps

and they slow down or stop

to gape at accidents.

I know I can never change their driving habits.

To understand them,

I only have to accept one fact.

They are all just like

a bunch of liberal democrats.

They come and go as they want

without facing any consequence.

It is their constitutional right

to exceed the speed limits.

And guess what? If anything happens.

If anything goes wrong.

Well, "It was all that big truck's fault."

They will always be right

and I will always be wrong.

SPATIAL RELATIONS

I must constantly analyze

the movement of the cars and trucks

in front of me,

on the other side of the truck wind screen.

Because it's all about our spatial relations.

Our stopping distance, our braking distance

and the speed of the cars in front of me

that really makes a difference.

I must constantly analyze this environment.

Because, if I give up and quit,

then any car that jumps in front of me

will have a high probability of being hit.

It is what is on the other side

of this piece of glass that matters to me most.

For if I should fail, more likely than not,

we will all be toast.

I must focus and concentrate

on the moving traffic in front of me

and analyze these spatial relations in my head

or very likely, in all probability,

we will end up dead.

QUICK QUIPS

It's an exercise in self control

to finish your job

and reach your goal.

It's an exercise that will allow your soul

to carry on without missing a step

throughout the direction your mind has set.

It will save you time and lower your speed

so you won't go to jail or talk to police.

To reach this mental state you must ignore

the trading of petty insults galore.

A calm peace in your mind you must restore.

and remove the irritations that are stored.

Nine times out of ten

your reaction goes back to childhood my friend.

Where you learned to stand your ground

and be a man.

You feel you must set them right.

They have disrespected you.

They did not treat you kind or right.

But still an insult so quickly lights

your first inclination, to stand and fight.

When someone says something mean

and you are certain they mean it.

You can just let it go.

That is always best you know.

To prevent the unkind greeting from smoldering

and catching fire inside your head.

You don't have to flip them a finger.

Be slick about it

and flip them a quick quip instead.

It will push them off balance mentally.

Then *they* will go down the road

with a hole burning in *their* head.

They will wonder and fantasize

about the quick response they could have said.

TWO EXPLOSIONS

I have to control my anger

and let it slip away.

I need to look out past the hood

to focus and concentrate.

For if I continue to grieve and think

of a personal confrontation,

or something mean that someone said

to raise a stink,

then I am going to end up dead.

For there will be two explosions.

And the first one will be

the silly fantasy in my head

because I am still mad

about something that was said.

Of course, explosion number two

will be when I drive my truck into

the cars that I failed to see,

the cars that are stopped in front of me

on the highway up ahead.

THE HIGH COST OF ANGER

They don't have to fight you.

They just say something snide

to put your head in a spin.

And you will be the one who does yourself in.

You will fantasize for the rest of the day

trying to figure out your favorite instant replay.

You will do it to yourself

and that is just what they want.

They achieved their objective.

They have rendered you totally ineffective.

And just what were you going to do

to this person who made fun of you?

Was it something demeaning that was said

that put a bug into your head?

You will lose your focus.

If you don't pay attention,

then you will run into

the next car that cuts in front of you.

You will never slow down.

You are bent on the fascination

of being bullied around.

After you've slammed into

the traffic that stopped in front of you,

vehicular homicide

or manslaughter will be your crime.

And what would you have done

to this person who made you

the object of their fun?

Would you beat them up?

Would you try to run over them with your truck?

It doesn't matter who said what

or what they said.

Anger has gotten into your head.

And like a child, you are going to play act it out.

You need to let it go right now.

It's the best thing to do.

You will never get even.

How many do you have to hospitalize

before you realize

how dangerous it is to let the fantasy play out?

BEHIND THE CLUSTER

It's raining down hard, brother.

Cats and dogs are in a downpour

and ten cars are jammed up

one behind the other.

Why are they driving along in a pile,

when there is no one behind us

for a quarter of a mile?

It's pouring down rain

and I can't believe

these dim wits in front of me

are packed up like sardines.

We slowed down twenty miles an hour

for these buckets of water.

And going fifty miles an hour is still insane,

but car drivers never tire of their reckless game.

Their habit of driving bumper to bumper

will never change.

They won't move over for the other guy

and they race down the road as if they could fly.

They think they can stop,

but they really cannot.

There is no tire friction in this rain

and, like a water skier, the cars hydroplane.

If they make a high speed maneuver

to swerve out of harm's way,

then they end up sliding down the road sideways.

They can't stop. They have all gone mad.

Just one wrong wiggle and it all goes bad.

Now there is one in the ditch and there goes another.

You would think they would make

more distance between their bumpers.

NOTHANKYOU@ REJECTION.COM

Now that I have a smart phone,

the world's greatest salesmen are calling my home.

Health insurance, car dealers and loan originators,

they never have quit calling me.

They try to plant a little seed

to make me think

they have something that I need.

Really, it is all about their greed.

They think more of their sales commission

than they think of me.

So I pay no attention to what they advertise.

I just skim to the bottom and click on unsubscribe.

That should stop them wouldn't you think,

with just a click on the unsubscribe link?

UP ON THE ROAD
HE STOOD

There was no doubt his stomach was in control.

His eyes were fixed on the road kill down below.

So he spiraled down and landed

on the edge of the road.

He hopped out into the middle of the street,

to sample his delicious treat.

He ruffled his wings and gave a little shriek.

Then he sank his beak into the tender meat.

He stood there enjoying his mid-morning snack.

He was certainly hungry, no doubt about that.

He was too big for the dumpster

at the fast food chain,

but that food is no good for him anyway.

He was on a hilltop or I might have swerved

into the other lane to miss the huge bird.

My horn was loud and it sounded three times.

And up popped the buzzard with his wings spread wide.

He hit the windshield hard.

I thought it knocked him unconscious.

His tongue was sticking out.

It was pretty obnoxious.

He looked me in the eye.

He was scrawny and mean.

He was an old buzzard just like me.

His life slipped away as he lay there.

When he slid off the hood

I shed a big tear.

I grieved and my heart sank.

It was just bad luck.

I would hate to sit down for dinner

and be hit by a truck.

BIG DELIVERY

I have a big delivery tomorrow morning.

And as the plan turns out,

driving through the city

is the shortest route.

Today is Sunday, much to my delight.

This drive through town is easy

because the traffic is so light.

The drivers have on their good behaviors.

They happily share the roads with their neighbors.

They drive straight to their church

to say their prayers and worship their Savior.

These courteous people, who drive the speed limit,

are on their way to church

to renew their vows and commitments.

They need redemption

to lift their souls and their spirits.

For last six days they have endured the devil.

The devil in their jobs.

The devil in their schools.

The devil of the politicians making stupid rules.

But on this seventh day,

it is time to move all evil out of the way.

Good Christians will bow down and pray.

They will tell the devil nay

and send the devil on his way.

They meditate on their goals and ambitions,

and they ask God for his guidance and forgiveness.

One day of worship against six of the bad.

That is how long the Lord's grace will last.

That's how strong renewing your vows can be.

If you accept the Lord's way and the Trinity.

It's time to cleanse the mind

and purify the heart.

A new week is coming.

It's time to make a fresh start.

So truckers, let's cleanse ourselves.

Grab your rosary.

We'll head off to the Trucker's Church

to say, "Hail Mary."

Fall down on your knees and you will be blessed.

We swear to drive courteous. We will do our best.

We will motor through the big towns easily

and we will be on time for our delivery.

WAKE UP HOSPITAL

I woke up in a hospital with plaster on my bones.

There was no pretty nurse and no phone to call home.

I don't remember what happened and I don't care to.

God kept me alive, and that certainly will do.

At the moment all I see are some IVs,

that drain into the needles that are stuck in me.

The very next thrill I believe I will see,

will be when the doctor lays

the hospital bill, on my chest,

in front of me.

As I recall, we were all bunched up

when two drivers steered for the same spot.

They bounced off each other more likely than not.

That's when the pile up began to happen

That is what started the chain reaction.

I thought I was a gonner and I steered for the shoulder.

I slid into the guard rail and I must have rolled over.

My memory is hazy. Everything was crazy.

I don't remember a thing,

and right now, I don't feel any pain.

If I had kept a big space in front of me,

I wouldn't be here.

I would be out on the road,

still shifting the gears.

I'd be driving on to my destiny.

The safest driver on earth I would be.

MR COCHISE MOUNTAIN

I was rolling down Mr. Cochise Mountain feeling nifty.

To save fuel, I was trying to coast past Mr. Swiftly.

I was enjoying the ride and having a good time,

when a flash of driver awareness

passed through my mind.

I looked in the mirror and I could see

a passenger car gaining on us rapidly.

So I tapped on the button for the jake.

And I put my foot lightly on the service brake.

As I slowed down and pulled in behind Mr. Swift,

a kid flipped me the finger, as a passing gift.

His silver car streaked right by me.

He must have been going a hundred and three.

In one more mile, where the road flattened out,

Sheriff Joe was parked in his favorite hideout.

He was hiding there in the vegetation

and when the kid screamed by,

Joe roared out without hesitation.

Joe's flashers were blazing.

If he caught the kid,

no doubt there would be some hazing.

Joe drove at a high speed to chase the kid down.

They went the distance, they raced all the way to town.

I'm sure Mr. Swift laughed just as hard as me.

As it turned out we were both blessed.

The kid accidentally took the heat for us.

You know, Sheriff Joe would have thrown

both of us under the bus.

CLIMBING THE HILLS AND GOING DOWN THE MOUNTAINS

To climb up the mountainside

I shift down from seven to six and then to five.

There is no other way around the hill

or out of this climb.

We have to pull the load to the top

and this is going to take some time.

Let the engine operate at optimum power.

To go up and down will take a whole hour.

Don't try to go faster than the engine can pull,

or else there's a gasket that you might blow.

Our speed is just a little faster than a man can run.

Let's enjoy the ride and try to have a little fun.

We will make it to the top against gravity.

So buckle up and try to enjoy the scenery.

At the top of the hill we will find

we must control our speed down the steep decline.

Don't go too fast or you will find

how easily you can lose 80,000 pounds

on the downhill side.

Check the speed and take it in stride.

Or else gravity will unleash a dangerous ride.

If we try to go fast, then we will roll.

Let's keep our 80,000 pounds under control.

45 miles per hour is the speed of this section,

so we put on the jake brake for added protection.

If you think you are in a hurry

and you have to go faster,

if a tight curve comes up,

it's gonna spell your disaster.

Rolling downhill at 100 miles an hour,

you can't stop on a dime.

And when the next curve comes up

you are going to find

the only way to stop your truck

is to crash into the mountainside.

If your brakes fade out, the cab will slow,

but the weight of the trailer will continue its roll.

As the speed of the trailer takes over the drive,

your cab will be pushed to the left or the right.

The trailer will drag your cab alongside,

and your rig will be in a classic jack knife.

To stay in control

you must drive slow.

Try to enjoy your ride.

There is no need to commit suicide.

Remember the rules of safety

when driving downhill in the rain, snow and ice.

Then you won't have to think twice

as you snake down the hill and through the canyon

twisting left and twisting right.

Sit back and relax,

and stay in low gear.

And you will make it back home

for Christmas this year.

Watch for smoke from the brakes

and watch your gauges.

And please don't be a candidate

for petty road rages.

Slow down, use caution

and take your time.

You will make it to the bottom

of the hill just fine.

You just have to be patient.

Keep your speed under forty five.

It is only time that you give up,

not your truck or your life.

Have discipline

and before you pucker up,

remember this little saying.

"Hardly a trucker is still alive,

who went down the hill

going more than fifty five."

THE 72ND ANNUAL CAR SHOW

People from all over New England attend

the National Car show in

Carlisle, Pennsylvania

and I can't blame them.

So, we are all here on the interstate

in a ten mile line,

and I will be 100 miles behind my delivery time

unless I can find a way to get around

this two mile an hour line.

I selected off duty

on the qual com driver log status.

I reached to the dash and I picked up the atlas.

I laid it on top of the steering wheel

and I tried to find a way out of this deal.

On the south side of town

there appeared to be a route.

If I could make it to Highway 11

I could bail myself out.

I rolled on the shoulder slowly

to the next exit ramp.

I had to be careful.

I almost hit a tramp.

I have to admit that I was nervous and scared.

Because part of the deal

to complete this sneak

is to pull a 53 foot trailer

through the tiny, narrow streets.

If the trailer is bigger than the streets are in town

it could be impossible to get turned around.

You don't take your trailer off a good route

on a whim or a lark,

cause when the sun goes down

you might still be parked.

To my surprise, on Highway 11,

there were two lanes in each direction.

This really relieved the one lane congestion.

I didn't get stuck or have to turn around.

And I did make it through the south side of town.

THE FUEL MANAGER

I got a call while I was driving the mountains

and valleys of New York and Pennsylvania.

The fuel manager called me today.

And he said,

"Bill your miles to the gallon are low.

You want them to be high you know.

If you would just accelerate slow,

you could save us thousands of dollars,

you know."

Then he added, "You know Bill,

saving fuel is saving the company money."

I replied to him, "Gosh, Mike.

You are making me feel guilty.

I know you want to make me a driver of reliability,

and sensible utility.

But, if I go any slower,

I'll have to pull off the road

and do my driving on the shoulder."

Mike emphasized,

"You are wasting our money

and that ain't funny.

So start saving fuel.

It's the same thing as saving

the company money!"

I replied, "Hey, Mike, give me a little credit

and cut me a little slack.

Surely you understand

that driving conditions vary throughout the land.

And you know, in the cities

there are always traffic jams."

I continued,

"Mike. I'm in the big city now.

I have to weave in in and out of the traffic congestion,

It gives me a headache

and a bad case of indigestion."

"I have to drive in the slow lane you know

and merge with the ramp traffic.

It is always stop and go.

Usually the cars are moving way too slow,

and you know,

that I have to move and go with the flow."

"Those car drivers are supposed

to smoothly slip into *my* lane,

but there are always two out of five

who are insane.

They always prove they have no brain.

They just don't give a damn.

They squeeze in front of me in traffic jams."

Then in all of his trucking wisdom Mike whispered,

"You are driving the big truck remember?

That is your legitimate excuse.

Let that other traffic be.

They got to wait for you.

Don't you see?"

Well, all of this was wearing me thin

I know the headquarters boys

and I hate to let them win.

They don't have to endure what we go through.

If they did, they would all be covered with tattoos.

I understand the manager has a job to do too.

But I wanted to tell him to go take a hike

and to go fly the company kite.

Instead, I said, "You know, Mike.

I think you are right

to help me with my low mileage plight.

But now I think

we are beginning to fight."

Mike replied right away.

"Now, Bill. Don't get all worked up.

I've done some research.

Your unit is able to get 8 miles to the gallon.

As long as you don't race up and down those hills

like you're a stallion."

I finally laughed the first time all day.

I asked him, "Just how old is that survey?"

And then I added, "If I drive slow,

I will be late for the delivery of goods

you know."

They won't give up.

They keep on bugging you.

He came back with a new question.

"Are you idling a lot?"

I denied it. I said, "No. I am not."

And then I remembered.

"Oh, yeah. Mike I forgot!

The APU is all messed up.

And now I have to run the AC off the idling truck.

Mike replied,

"Well, that will do it. When you get back in town,

get that APU fixed. That is high priority,

You shouldn't run the AC on maximum cool.

If you do you are a fool,

but that is still not the problem.

Turn the AC off and roll your windows down."

Now this comment crawled right under my skin,

and so I said to him,

"I know what it is. I just remembered.

Saving fuel is not gonna happen.

I guess the company is just out of luck.

Yesterday the turbo just fell off the truck."

And I hung up.

EPILOGUE

THE WOOD STOVE

The cold frozen moisture fell from the clouds into the sky.

The light flakes appeared from out of nowhere.

Wrapped in our blanket on the swing,

we sat and watched the wind blow the snow

horizontally into our faces.

Soon we were dusted from head to foot

with large fluffy flakes.

We are warm, in our bodies and our minds and our hearts.

We hold each other's hands as we sit on the porch swing.

And the driver spoke to his wife,

"I am here just to tell you these stories.

I hope they made you smile.

I just stopped by to talk and laugh with you awhile."

She leaned close to her husband and whispered in his ear.

"If you leave now, you will be in big trouble.

I need you to clear a path through the snow for me

tomorrow. You can prove to me that you are as strong as

the day I married you."

He looked into her beautiful eyes and answered, "Of

course, my love. I will clear a path for your lovely feet.

I am here to do chores for you and to do your bidding.

But first I will require a cup of hot tea. Or better yet,

a hot buttered rum."

She smiled at him with her heart and her mind as she said

"Why don't we go inside and get out of the wind?"

"That is a wonderful idea," he said.

She replied. "And I will require your attention on the floor

by the wood stove. And then It will be off to bed.

As long as you split your lotto winnings with me.

She bumped her head to his. Her signal for a kiss.

THE END

APPENDIX

THE ENRAGED STUDENT AND THE DRIVING INSTRUCTOR

"Slow down!"

Sean shouted out a warning. He enjoyed handing them out. He enjoyed helping the student drivers. Actually, this time he was criticizing John's driving. For John Coles, this happened to be the 536th time. It was the straw that pushed John over the edge.

The speed of the truck picked up. Sean was looking ahead. The truck was rapidly approaching a deceleration ramp with a tight 270 degree turn. Shawn yelled this time. It was both a demand and a plea.

"I said slow down! You are going too fast for this exit!" Yet the speed increased again and Sean turned his head to the student to see if John Coles had lost his mind.

What he saw took him aback and scared the life right out of him. For in the driver seat was no longer the student Coles.

Aaaaaaaaaaaaaaaaaaaa! Ahhh! Sean screamed! Aaaaaaaaaaaaaaaaaaaaagggghhh!

A large Grim Reaper sat across from him. He was hooded and caped. His eye sockets were pitch black except for two bright red, laser pupil dots that stared menacingly at Sean. A large scythe leaned against the driver seat.

"Did you say too fast?" the Grim Reaper asked with a wide and surly grin. He flashed his beady red eyes directly at Sean and he brayed, "I don't need to brake! Sean! Pay Attention! I am about to show you the proper speed for tight, consecutive three hundred and sixty degree turns!"

Sean said nothing. He was filled with fear.

"Slow down to thirty you say? Awwwwwwwwwwwwwww. That's no fun. What do say we do one hundred fifty for this tight funnel turn coming up?"

Sean was held speechless and frozen in place.

"So, do you want to see the proper speed for the tight 360 degree turns?" The Reaper yelled again, "Speak up, boy!"

"I guess you better hang onto your seat, Sean! Hang on to your seat!" The Reaper commanded. He threw back his head and began to laugh. It turned into a continuously roaring, frightful howl.

Goose bumps and fear rippled in waves through Sean's body and mind. Sean shivered and his hair stood on end.

The Grim Reaper cranked the wheel and stomped on the gas. The truck twisted ninety degrees as if it was a test tube in a centrifuge.

Round and round they went in a tight little circle. The speed increased instantly to two hundred miles an hour.

Sean was slammed down fast to his seat. His face was contorted beyond recognition. He felt like he weighed 1000 pounds. Everything outside the truck was one big swirl of different colors.

It was all Sean could do to turn his neck. He could see the Grim Reaper floating gently, weightlessly, just above the driver seat. An outrageous smile was on his face. The cape billowed around him.

The Grim Reaper threw his head back and roared with glee. It warmed his heart to make Sean pee. And they continued to spin in animation until Sean passed out.

That morning, Sean woke up and got out of the top bunk quietly, not to disturb his student. He was edgy. He couldn't quite figure out why he felt slow and heavy. He couldn't remember where they were or how they got there. He must have fallen asleep.

Suddenly he recalled the bad dream he had. He turned to the bottom bunk and shook his student John Coles awake. "You would not believe the dream I had last night."

John Coles opened his eyes. They were two tiny slits. The pupils were laser red. "What dream? John laughingly said. Why have you been sleeping so long?"

Then all of a sudden John disappeared. It was the Grim Reaper who lay in John's bed.

Sean spun around. He jumped on the passenger seat and kicked the passenger door open.

With a loud scream he leapt from the truck and ran through the truck stop.

He was never seen again.

Now it is time to say no more, the long day is at an end.

It's time for sleep and a bit of peace, so that we can mend.

And tomorrow awake to continue our work

with hope and trust in the Lord.

ABOUT THE AUTHOR

Bill Overmyer drove in military convoys in Iraq as a contract driver for five years. He hauled equipment, supplies, vehicles, MRAPS, humvees, SUVS, tanks, water, JP8 and the mail. Bill currently works in the oil fields in North Dakota.

Printed in the United States
by Baker & Taylor Publisher Services